DRAWER OF LETTERS

Ricky Monahan Brown is a writer and poet living in Edinburgh. His memoir, *Stroke: A 5% chance of survival*, was a Scotsman Nonfiction Book of 2019. The spoken word event he co-founded, *Interrobang?!* won the 2017 Saboteur Award for Best Regular Spoken Word Night in Britain. His debut fiction collection, *Terminal*, was published by Sincere Corkscrew in 2024.

Also by Ricky Monahan Brown

Terminal (Sincere Corkscrew, 2024)

Little Apples (Leamington Books, 2022)

Stroke: A 5% Chance of Survival (Sandstone Press, 2019)

CONTENTS

FREIGHT TRAINS	9
DRAWER	10
L'ÉTRANGER	12
MOONBEAMS	16
TWO COFFEES	18
FIVE HAIKU	20
UMAMI	21
LADY SLIPPER	22
INNA GADDA	24
THE BALLAD OF CENN FÁELAD MAC AILELLA	25
E PLURIBUS UNUM, EX UNO MULTIS	28
GOOSEBERRIES / CREAM	29
DE-COMPOSITION	31
CALEDONIA	32
DOING AWAY	33
FIVE MORE HAIKU	34
SOME VOID	35
JACOB'S LADDER	37
THE BONFIRE	39
ACKNOWLEDGMENTS	41

To Beth

© 2025, Ricky Monahan Brown. All rights reserved. No part of this book may be reproduced, stored in a retrieval system, or transmitted in any form or by any means, whether electronic, mechanical, photocopying, recording, or otherwise, without the prior written permission of the publisher, except in the case of brief quotations used in reviews or scholarly works.

This work may not be used for text and data mining, including (without limitation) the training of artificial intelligence technologies or systems. The author and publisher expressly reserve all rights and opt out of any applicable text and data mining exceptions.

ISBN: 978-1-917617-51-2

Cover designed by Aaron Kent

Cover illustration: © oksenoyd_irina / Adobe Stock

Edited and Typeset by Aaron Kent

The author has asserted their right to be identified as the author of this Work in accordance with the Copyright, Designs and Patents Act 1988.

Broken Sleep Books Ltd
PO BOX 102
Llandysul
SA44 9BG

Drawer of Letters

Ricky Monahan Brown

Broken Sleep Books

FREIGHT TRAINS

On industrial carpeted hallway
Fill a small plastic bucket with ice
Let the spring-loaded door guillotine
All the things that were treasured before

Then, enveloped in functional cotton
Think of all of the things that were lost
In the cattle class over the ocean
With the other folks panning for gold

Now this bed stretches off to the TV
Like the plains stretching off like freight trains
And the newsreaders tell me that Camden
Will be blazing all night long again

And the man who I heard sold the world is
Falling down to the Earth on the tube
I am so far from home and I weep
For the things that I have set on fire

DRAWER

a drawer made of letters

letters made of lined paper
letters made of hand-cut paper
letters made of thick Egyptian sheets
letters made of translucent skin

letters bound by bulldog clips
letters secured by steely staples
letters gathered by woven strings
letters stuck by elastic gum bands

letters woken by a slashing pen
letters leavened by a smiling blot
letters smudged by a dragging hand
letters blurred by *<illegible>*

letters built by paragraph slabs
paragraphs formed from frilly sentences
sentences verbed into brief existence
verbs that describe a life

and a letter made of words
made of letters

like L

and E

and A

and V

L'ÉTRANGER

I.

It's strange,

Maman est mort, and next our marriage, too.
Soon you and I will be estranged. Funny
That word's only for families and spouses.
Now mum is dead, who gives a shit how I feel?
The people who were meant to, never did.

We always spoke two different languages.
Nous ne parlons pas comme nous l'avons fait
I said, but you always had a reply
To whatever question you thought you heard:
So take the trash out. But I tried that. I...

...tried everything. Warning and surprise.
On Valentine's Day, you showed me your feelings.
A present, red like cartoon hearts or passion.
A desultory drill for me to fix
Myself up. I always was a project.

II.

Got someone in to do the structural work.
She didn't know it was a full redo.
Took me on as a bit of fun, not knowing
The job would be two lifetimes' full of care.

The ruins were preserved, a memorial,
But something new was built from the ashes.
Recognisable, yes, but forward-looking;
Founded on Narragansett Pier Granite.

So I didn't collapse, but mum did, died.
She saw a picture of my next wife — once.
I wanted her to know that someone cared
Who didn't think I was all that damaged.

I thought there was a flash of recognition.
She didn't say, but saw the subway platform
The station seconds of interaction
Too late, another messed muscle; missed call.

Leading my reputation to the gallows,
I wanted the people to cheer and spit
In the face of the thing they could not have.
But now I see their love of love reflected.

III.

The colour of the sand is the colour
Of Algerian sun is the colour
Of your plain simple dress is the colour
Of the klieg lights that mark out the border

Of passing from that life to the new life
Where salt seas surely signal us to swim;
Float amidst the ever-changing currents
That feel this moment. And this moment, too.

Where salt and sand and sun and sea and sex
Blend, mature, into a kick in the chest;
Subtle and fragrant and to be savoured
Anew each time, a new kaleidoscope.

Colours reflected, the swell of the sea
That moulds and outlasts both empires and dance
For all is transient, even the sea;
But not this moment. And not this moment.

IV.

Which is approximated as static
At some other time scale where matter flows
Down density ropes to the node-like wells
Where it collects in places where stuff is.

What fills up the ropes? And how does the stuff
Get out of the wells? It doesn't get out.
The ropes just started and have been trickling
Since ten to the minus thirty-seven.

So even the cosmos sort of only
Gets that one shot at it basically
And this second shot is my only shot
Filling node-like wells with infinite love.

MOONBEAMS

It's morning, the dark's behind us
Thrushes thunder morning chorus
Millions of tons — exploding sun —
Silently stalk the horizon

I want to get closer and hear
But a vast stone blanket of sky
Muffles furious life and fear
Below where the little birds fly

Nothing can be the same again
Touching her each night in my dreams
I had that long curve in my hand
Standing in the spring of moonbeams

And I want to be your Laika
At the edge, falling forever
And orbiting just like Yuri
Beyond the human boundary

Pierce that thick corporeal veil
Once around, two, three, and then
Returning from the celestial
What comes after you've been John Glenn?

Mercury escorts Larunda
With love of glistening quicksilver
Makes way for Leucothea's beau
Bringer of plague, proud Apollo

But being a mortal Apollo
Who sees the long curve of the Earth
Has the hardest act to follow
With no need to prove any worth

So I choose not the lunar leap
Years of fiery climb, descent deep
Instead I prove manly mettle
Skipping straight to Aldrin's bottle

Nothing can be the same again
Touching her each night in my dreams
I had that long curve in my hand
Standing in the spring of moonbeams

TWO COFFEES

The door frame composes a picture,
Presses pause, and imposes an order.
In this bomb site of neglected room,
Your hair explodes in Mandelbrot bloom
Across a blank canvas.

I stand in the doorway and linger
With the red button under my finger.
Press, and everything stops in its place —
Atoms only vibrate in all of space
Throughout a cold cosmos.

While you're still in the arms of Morpheus
I can count iotas for each of us
A one-night stand, times three-sixty-five,
Times all the years we'll both be alive,
The echoes after death.

Like atoms, they reach infinity.
To count them would take an eternity:
Time for the boy in front of the telly;
Time to learn how you prefer your coffee,
Or if it's tea you want.

Imagine coffee grounds in the press
Tang of orange and mud, smoky and fresh.
Brownian motion, sugary swirls.
In an ocean of coffee, the cream curls;
Flavours tweak and adjust.

But today, I'm not that good at maths,
Can't freeze atoms, or read futures' paths.
The scene doesn't reflect well on me,
Running down the street for a pack of three
While you read the bookshelves.

Our chance isn't serendipity, but
The dumb luck of chaotic theory.
I know I'm a repeating fraction
Who hopes you'll round me up into the one
Allowed to stay around.

And the way I could show I could care
Was standing quietly, patiently there:
One black coffee of hot calm order,
One frothy latté of blended discord.
I don't know which is yours.

FIVE HAIKU

umbrellas birling
stop
then flower

                                        seasonal gales
                                           batter glass
                                  seeking equilibrium

                  puddles sparkle
                  on piebald walls

heavy wet sun
illuminates pillow hair

                                      autumnal silence:
                                    ambient birdsong
                                    windswept words

UMAMI

Smells of liquid smoke flood the fluid flat
To give the pulses the tang of notmeat;
Not meat, but the opposite — life, slow-cooked,
Chewy, and ready for mastication.
Like a life, or a rehydrated soul.

I tear seitan in twain, then rend my flesh,
So letting you see the empty chambers.
You abhor the vacuum and fill me not
With words, but with thoughts, and I am nourished
Not sated, so that later I hear reds
As I tear your flesh with teeth to be
Smashed by the iron your lifeblood provides.

LADY SLIPPER

I awake from the us
ual, dark, dread
sleep in an empty room; this va
cant bed still full of you. My
arms,

too — full of you. My nose,
my mouth. Then
you rush out when consciousness sid
les suddenly in. *So* I
chase,

fling my face into your
pillow, which
still smells of that fresh smell that you
love. You love that. And my heart
leaps

yet again. But still. No
you. So. On
a delicate wrist, I apply
your perfume — *The Orchid*. Not
the

one that we smelled at the
orchid show.
No. That stank of carrion to
attract the pollinators,
all

yellowblack dangers. This,
sticky, slight,
delicate. The cool, sweet scent of
the hot, damp jungle. The jun
gle

that mingles with our skin.
And as the
sunshower pours we are toge
ther again. But still. No you.
So.

INNA GADDA

My grandfather's garden still seems the same:
So orderly, still set in those six squares.
Is it so strange that this is where I came
To escape a hard world of earthly cares?
Sandy coastal soil runs through my fingers
And measures the time that is left for me.
Yes, life is hard, but I choose to linger;
I could stay here for an eternity.
And an ocean away, my body lies,
Left arm tingles, that side is insensate.
What I once knew is that all lives must die;
That body in a disunited state,
Its nerves decay, leaving a feeling that
Life hangs suspended like Schrödinger's cat.

THE BALLAD OF CENN FÁELAD MAC AILELLA

The last thing I see is a cairn
   Take the earth in my hand
The air smells wet, the stone has heft
   But earth crumbles like sand

A disaster is playing out
   Thousands of miles away
There, you're murmuring a promise
   Here, rocks in disarray

Survive and I take the pebble
   Like one of my forebears
But the mountains crowd grimly in
   Rain breaks the Glen Coe air

The light goes out but I can see
   Your garnet eyes aflame
I know I'll climb over my corpse
   To see you one more time

The mist is heavy with the souls
   Of men who went to bed
Expecting to dine with their chief
   The chief, the men are dead

Coming from the Devil's Staircase
    A sword blow splits my skull
Springing heather's wetted by my
    Fluid, blood, dark and dull

I go offline, you think you know
    You won't see me again
I can't forget and I forget
    My helper and my friend

In each new morning passing by
    There should be hope and yet
In undetermined dawn and dusk
    Broke in an oubliette

I can't name you, make memories real
    The mood becomes maudlin
So light a candle in your heart
    Till we can laugh again

Guttering flickers of rational thought
    Are sparked by that tallow
The rains move on, the winds fall low
    Keep flames alive and blow

One day, thousands of miles away

   Dispense a loving smile

Gaze down from wisdom hard won, say:

   Took your stone from the pile.

E PLURIBUS UNUM, EX UNO MULTIS

It's true, this land contains its multitudes.
See it change through highway-driven hours:
Concrete jungles, tree-like cellphone towers,
Then honest-to-god, plant-based, wooden woods
Within which woods this man-made orchard hides,
Where we go to escape the urban sprawl,
Forced by our circumstance to leave it all,
Betrayed by flesh and fortune's waning tides,
Emerging here, to waken up anew.
Embrace nature with all the privilege
Reserved for enforced idlers and the rich.
Perhaps bad luck was best for me and you:
Open windows and hobble out the door,
To hope fortune will favour us once more.

Maybe we've escaped the smoke of the crash
Maybe we're shielded from the king's mist
Maybe we're far from the fog of war

GOOSEBERRIES / CREAM

1. Gooseberries

The future house is modern, stark yet warm.
Metal, corrugated, is insulated
By moss that could instead cover the blocks
Of peat that heat the hearth with redolent
Smoke where remembered malts of Brooklyn meld
Our senses in forgotten moments that
Still paint a picture that hangs light in our home.

I tell you this and you pause, pierce the skin
Of tough, succulent gooseberry, fleshy
And juicy, too — a juice that floods your mouth
And runs right down your chin that laughs along
With limpid eyes and cherry cheeks as well.

2. Cream

The old house, solid, saved me — anchored life
To Buckie, where I can still smell the salt
That comes back across Atlantic current
But can't corrode containers holding all
We've collected — not a lot; but still
Enough to fill two floors with all the smells
That I recall. The whisky, of course,
But also sweet meringues and sugared cream
Adorned by gooseberries, tasting of love.

DE-COMPOSITION

           up on high
        hanging in the sultry sky
   leaving all of you too paralysed
   amid too many threats to analyse
   silent spores spread settle seep
      over humans' silent sleep
           below
           below
           below
           below
           below
           below
   and   below even that   to
meet another   mushroom cloud that extends under
past your understanding – to the evolutionary step beyond

CALEDONIA

200 million years ago, I read
Scotland had been a desert.
Then I left forever that Caledonia,
A country become a land looking backwards,
A sentimental song sketched on a beer mat on a beach

Sure enough, as we fly over
The filigree fingerling fjords of the Forth,
My old home is no more.
The friendly clearances – and mum's departure – have seen to that,
Even though I recognize my old da,
A different man, but still an anchor to the harbour below.
On the edge of the new old world, I am scared.
Over 16 years, I traversed the old new world,
And by the time I was through,
We were an entirely new group of people.
I am changed, too —
My sandstone heart broken, yet held together by succulent American oak.
So, as I survey this new land, I have strength.
You brought me back from Buckie,
And, my Charon, you sailed me safely across the Styx
So I returned from the underworld alive
Even though I had no coin for you, and owe you everything.

Now, as we stand shoulder to shoulder on this remote peninsula,
Scotland may be gone,
But this Caledonia is my adventure with you.

DOING AWAY

It's not raining, but it's not not raining.
To the east
a flag blue sky empty of omens.
To the west
cumulonimbi solidly form, piling on
until they're scraping the top of the sky.
There's something coming
But how can we talk about death when delicately
you're scheduled for an endoscopy
not a colonoscopy

In eerie silence, thoughts
scramble over each over until the gusts
tumult in from the coast.
The gale tattooing my eardrums
drowned out by anticipatory skirling laments
What is my elegy? Forty years
and I don't know this man whose name I share.
Three times I ask, *How are you doing?*
hoping you'll answer to shut me up

But you've found the words that convey less meaning than
Not bad, Awright
If sharing leaves you exposed, then your footprints
skitter away with the Silverknowes sands
How am I doing? you say
Och, doing away.

FIVE MORE HAIKU

under static skies
trees huddle, waiting

                                            clouds linger
                                              diffusing
                                    bright autumn light

                  one million from one
                  and e unibus pluram
                  kaleidoscopic

broken blackbird hops
through industrial estate
to postage stamp green

                                  size and age mean naught
                                  to the towering bonsai
                                  who just wants to be

SOME VOID

Sometimes he'd like the world to know
He enjoys the morning chorus
Even if it thinks he prefers
Killers crushing pointy wee skulls
Under big pointy cowboy boots.

Enjoying sweet white wine's good too.

He thinks of George Perec's novel
Which doesn't use the letter e.
Thinks of the gift of not writing
Mère or père or première épouse
Or deuxième or troisième

Or even his own moniker.

Consuelo does his pedicure.
This isn't some future hellworld
Or murderous bloodthirsty present.
He thinks he'd prefer plum polish.
Something suited to his skin tone?

Consuelo gossips on ignored,

Gossips while he thinks of dying,
Not like in those bogus stories,
Wishes for end without the guts
For it, though he knows the horror
Of presenting like some monster.

He'd prefer to tell this story.

The story of an unknown man
Who knows not of self-expression,
But knows that moral choice defines
Him and the men who're just like him,
And when he fails like all men must

Finds consolation where he can.

JACOB'S LADDER

Bianca Clifton died, November sixth
In 1890, one year, four days old.
Now long encrypted in the underworld
Beneath a grassy Greenwood, Brooklyn hill.

Now annually, I come to visit her,
Dark and damp tunnels almost lit by skylight.
The happy screams of living kids too much,
I claw towards the sun, and gasp for air.

Emerging from the Greenwood catacombs,
Mists rolling east surround me, leaving just
The Fields of Asphodel beyond the pale,
That foggy place where sunshine never shows

Till Scots of Civil War present escort,
And we clamber onto Jacob's Ladder
To Nelson's towering upturned telescope
That peers into the ground, declaring home.

Inside, the whitewash painted spiral says
So early, *Almost there, Keep going on*
On steps all counterclockwise, sword hands free
One hundred forty three the skyward stairs.

Shrieking shades assault ancient window panes
Until, at last, a door so thin and blue,
Explodes in raining shards of steely hue
To fall on souls assembled far below.

THE BONFIRE

I limp to a spring wake. The smoke of dead
Plant matter burning nostril hair alive.
It's time to pile the corpses on the pyre;
The friends and friends of friends who failed long winter.

Though smoke spirals and stings my eyes, I peer
Into the murk where sparks and cinders reel,
While behind me, death rattles wheeze and hobble
Off stage to let limbering life extend

Towards the future, where a cobalt sky
Is shining light on hopeless, darkened pasts.
I know that all too soon an inky void
Extinguishes the flames, and so today

    — Let's dance.

ACKNOWLEDGMENTS

Ricky would like to acknowledge the platform and inspiration offered by his comrades Stephanie and Paul in the Nerd Bait band, as well as by Barbara Melville and Illicit Ink, especially with respect to the poem *Moonbeams*.

Particular thanks are due to Paul Walker for supplying the words and ideas explored in Part IV of *L'Étranger*.

LAY OUT YOUR UNREST

www.ingramcontent.com/pod-product-compliance
Lightning Source LLC
LaVergne TN
LVHW041311080426
835510LV00009B/954